marie claire

sweet

acknowledgements

Firstly, I wish to thank Anne Wilson, Kay Scarlett and Mark Smith for allowing me to expand this wonderful series. To the doesn't-miss-a-trick talents of Jane Price, who makes writing so much easier for me. To Marylouise Brammer for providing the finishing touches as only she can. A baker's dozen basketful of thank you's to my peas-in-a-pod kitchen buddy Valli Little who tested, tasted and tweaked and put such a special part of herself into preparing these recipes for photography; thank you also for allowing me to use your glorious home for this book. To Michelle, my stylist, for giving this book the gift of her immense talent and softness, and Chris for the divine photographs. To Anna Waddington for her supreme organization.

To my family for their continued support and encouragement; Penel, Michael, Shem and Gabe for all that is unconditional; Kerry Spence for being such a wonderful mentor and all my friends for their love, patience and never-ending acceptance of their guinea pig status.

To the Antico family for getting what needs to be got, even when it is a seasonal impossibility.

To all of you who buy these books, a huge thank you—I hope you enjoy cooking from them as much as I enjoy writing them. This one is for Jude, my patient and loyal friend who is always there for a beer, bubbly, bickie or burger. And lastly, to Bilgola—bless you for keeping me sane.

The publisher wishes to thank the following for their generosity in supplying props for the book: Pigott's Store; Orson and Blake; The Bay Tree; Orrefors Kosta Boda; Feast; Royal Doulton; Waterford Wedgwood; Shack; Bison Homewares; Breville; Ordal; Porters Paints and Mud Australia.

Front cover: passionfruit custard pots, page 50

marie claire

sweet

jody vassallo

MURDOCH
B O O K S

contents

Sometimes the sweetest thing is a
wonderfully simple idea that can be
put together in seconds. Try...

sheets of puff pastry, cut into strips and
sprinkled with coconut before baking

slices of dried fruit, sprinkled with brown
sugar and grilled until it caramelizes

a scoop of ice cream in a chocolate
waffle cone pressed with gold leaf

a spoonful of clotted cream with just
about anything you can think of

sheep's milk yoghurt with puréed
strawberries stirred through

melted chocolate piped or drizzled into
shapes on baking paper and left to set

thick home-made custard, laced with a
good dash of your favourite liqueur

glasses of cardamom caffe latte with a
generous nip of frangelico

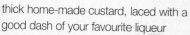

mixed nuts in honey swirled through
softened French vanilla ice cream

shapes of honeydew, rock melon and
watermelon threaded onto skewers

festive white and redcurrants or cherries
set in small squares of jelly

roses and lavender, lightly brushed with
egg whites and rolled in caster sugar

glasses of cold milk with spoons dipped in melted chocolate and chopped nuts

cups of ginger tea with lemongrass swizzle sticks

warm shots of fruit-flavoured schnapps with a white cherry dropped in

wontons lightly brushed with butter, baked and sprinkled with icing sugar

The 'Italian trifle' can also be made
in individual portions—serve in
glasses so you can see the layers.

tiramisu

3 eggs, separated
1/2 cup caster sugar
250 g (8 oz) mascarpone
300 ml (10 fl oz) cream
2 cups strong black coffee, cooled
1/4 cup brandy
1 packet (300 g/10 oz) large
sponge finger biscuits
50 g (1³/4 oz) dark chocolate,
finely grated

Put the egg yolks and sugar in a bowl
and beat until thick and pale. Add the
mascarpone and beat until smooth.
Beat the egg whites in a clean dry bowl
until soft peaks form, then fold into the
mascarpone mixture.
Beat the cream until soft peaks form,
then fold into the mixture.
Combine the coffee and brandy in a
small bowl. Dip the biscuits, one at a
time and fairly quickly, into the coffee
and arrange over the base of a
25 x 20 cm shallow dish. Top with half
the mascarpone mixture.
Repeat with another layer of biscuits
and the remaining mascarpone mixture.
Cover with plastic wrap and refrigerate
for 4 hours. Sprinkle with grated
chocolate before serving.

Serves 8–10

rhubarb and mango custard ice cream

Put the rhubarb, 3 tablespoons water and half the sugar in a pan, cover and cook over medium heat for 5–10 minutes or until soft. Transfer to a bowl and leave to cool.

Beat half the cream until soft peaks form, then refrigerate until ready to use. Put the remaining cream in a pan and heat until it is about to boil.

Put the egg yolks, vanilla, custard powder and remaining sugar in another pan, add the hot cream and whisk to combine. Return to the heat and stir constantly until the custard thickens. Stir in the mango and whipped cream then transfer to an ice-cream machine and churn until frozen.

(Alternatively, pour the mixture into a large metal container, cover and freeze for 2 hours, until setting around the edge. Scrape into a bowl and beat until smooth. Pour back into the clean metal container, cover and freeze until firm.)

Soften a little and swirl through the rhubarb. Keep frozen but soften in the fridge for 30 minutes before serving.

250 g (8 oz) rhubarb stalks, chopped
1 cup caster sugar
600 ml (20 fl oz) cream
3 egg yolks
1 teaspoon vanilla essence
2 teaspoons custard powder
500 g (1 lb) puréed mango flesh

Serves 8

Chocolate boosts the endorphin
levels in our brain, which is why
most of us are unable to resist.

chocolate and frangelico mousse

250 g (8 oz) dark chocolate
1 tablespoon golden syrup
3 egg whites
2 egg yolks
1/4 cup frangelico
100 ml (3 1/2 fl oz) cream

Put the chocolate in a heatproof bowl
over a pan of simmering water, making
sure the base of the bowl is not sitting
in the water. Leave until the chocolate
has melted. Remove and allow to cool
slightly, then stir in the golden syrup.
Beat the egg whites in a clean dry bowl
until stiff peaks form. Stir the egg yolks
and frangelico into the cool chocolate.
Beat the cream until soft peaks form.
Gently fold the cream and egg whites
into the chocolate with a large metal
spoon or spatula.
Pour the chocolate mousse into serving
bowls or cups and refrigerate until firm.

Serves 4

Botrytis is the mould that forms on the grapes used for these intensely sweet dessert wines.

fruits in sweet wine

Wash the fruits and allow to dry completely, then arrange in a large serving bowl.
Put the wine, vanilla, saffron and cardamom pods in a pan and heat gently for 5 minutes. Set aside and leave to infuse and cool for 10 minutes.
Pour the cooled liquid over the fruits, cover and refrigerate for 4 hours, turning every couple of hours to ensure all the fruits have marinated in the wine.
Serve with fresh goat's milk yoghurt drizzled with a little golden syrup.

Serves 6–8

250 g (8 oz) cherries, stalks attached
250 g (8 oz) strawberries
2 peaches, cut into wedges
500 g (1 lb) watermelon, peeled and cut into triangles
200 g (6 1/2 oz) redcurrants
200 g (6 1/2 oz) grapes
375 ml bottle botrytis wine
1 vanilla bean, halved
2 pinches saffron threads
2 cardamom pods, bruised
200 g (6 1/2 oz) goat's milk yoghurt
2 tablespoons golden syrup

Ginger has been adding spice for many years—legend has the first gingerbread made in 2400 BC.

upside-down pear and ginger cake

80 g (2³/₄ oz) butter, melted
1/2 cup brown sugar
2 x 800 g (1 lb 10 oz) cans pears in natural juice, drained and quartered
250 g (8 oz) butter
1/2 cup demerara sugar
1/2 cup treacle
1/2 cup golden syrup
2 teaspoons bicarbonate of soda
3¹/₂ cups plain flour
1 tablespoon ground ginger
2 teaspoons ground allspice
2 eggs, lightly beaten

Preheat the oven to 180°C (350°F/ Gas 4). Grease and line a 24 cm (10 inch) square cake tin. Pour melted butter over the base and sprinkle with brown sugar. Put the pears, cut side down, around the edge of the tin. Put the butter, demerara sugar, treacle, golden syrup and 1 cup water in a pan and stir over low heat until completely dissolved. Bring to the boil.
Remove from the heat and stir in the bicarbonate of soda. Cool slightly.
Sift the flour, ginger and allspice into a bowl and make a well in the centre. Add the eggs to the butter mixture and pour into the well. Stir to just combine. Spoon carefully over the pears and bake for 1 hour or a little longer, until a skewer comes out clean when inserted into the centre of the cake.

Serves 8–10

Granita is ice cream without cream.
The mixture is frozen without
churning so the crystals are rough.

melon margarita granita

Put the honeydew melon in a blender with the lime juice, sugar and tequila and process until smooth. Season to taste with salt.

Pour into a shallow metal container, cover and freeze for 2 hours, or until just frozen around the edges. Scrape with a fork to break up any ice crystals, then return to the freezer for another hour. Repeat the freezing and scraping five times over the next 3–4 hours, or until the granita is frozen into evenly sized ice crystals.

Rub teaspoons with lime and then coat lightly with salt.

Serve the granita with the salted spoons to be stirred through.

Serves 4–6

600 g (1 1/4 lb) honeydew melon, seeds removed, roughly chopped
1/4 cup lime juice
1/2 cup caster sugar
80 ml (2 3/4 fl oz) tequila
1 lime, cut into wedges
sea salt

Pandan (screw pines) grow on tropical coasts. More conveniently, the leaves are sold at Asian markets.

black sticky rice

1 1/2 cups black glutinous rice
2 pandan leaves
1/2 cup grated dark palm sugar
pinch of salt
1/2 cup coconut cream

Soak the rice in cold water overnight. Rinse thoroughly and drain. Put the rice and the knotted pandan leaves in a pan with 1.5 litres water and bring to the boil. Reduce the heat and simmer for 30–40 minutes.
Add the palm sugar and salt and simmer for another 20–25 minutes, or until the rice is soft.
Spoon into cups or bowls and drizzle with a little coconut cream.

Serves 4–6

Hazelnut meal is now often found in supermarkets, though you could replace it with almond meal.

raspberry marshmallow friands

Preheat the oven to 200°C (440°F/ Gas 6). Grease 10 friand tins with butter. Sift the flour and icing sugar into a bowl. Stir in the hazelnut meal and coconut. Whisk the egg whites in a clean dry bowl until foamy. Fold into the dry ingredients with the melted butter. Set aside 20 of the raspberries, then carefully fold the rest into the mixture with the chopped marshmallows. Spoon into the tins.

Press a halved marshmallow and two raspberries into the top of each friand. Bake for 20 minutes, or until golden and starting to come away from the sides of the tins. Leave to cool for 5 minutes in the tins before turning out onto a wire rack to cool completely.

Makes 10 friands

1 cup plain flour
1 1/2 cups icing sugar
100 g (3 1/2 oz) hazelnut meal
1/2 cup desiccated coconut
5 egg whites
180 g (6 oz) butter, melted and cooled
100 g (3 1/2 oz) raspberries
50 g (1 3/4 oz) small pink marshmallows, chopped
10 small pink marshmallows, extra

lemon and lime tart with red papaya

Pastry
2 cups plain flour
2 tablespoons icing sugar
150 g (5 oz) butter, chopped

Filling
2 eggs
3 egg yolks
1/2 cup caster sugar
1/2 cup lemon juice
1/4 cup lime juice
2 tablespoons lemon rind
2 teaspoons lime rind
100 ml (3 1/2 fl oz) cream
1–2 small red papaya, sliced
lime juice and icing sugar, to serve

Preheat the oven to 200°C (400°F/ Gas 6). Sift the flour and icing sugar into a bowl and rub in the butter with your fingertips until the mixture resembles fine breadcrumbs. Add 2 tablespoons of iced water and mix with a flat-bladed knife until the dough comes together. Gather into a ball, cover with plastic wrap and refrigerate for 10 minutes. Roll out on a lightly floured surface until large enough to cover the base and side of a shallow 22 cm (9 inch) round loose-bottomed flan tin. Line the pastry with baking paper and fill with baking beads or uncooked rice. Bake for 10 minutes, then remove the beads and paper and bake for 10 minutes, or until the pastry is dry and golden.
Reduce the oven to 160°C (315°F/ Gas 2–3). Whisk the eggs, yolks and sugar until pale, add the juices, rinds and cream and whisk together.
Pour into the pastry base and bake for 35–45 minutes or until set. Leave for 30 minutes, then top with papaya, a squeeze of lime juice and icing sugar.

Serves 6–8

Vienna almonds are sugar-coated almonds. If you can't find them, use sugar-coated peanuts.

chocolate almond ponds

Preheat the oven to 200°C (400°F Gas 6). Lightly grease four 1 1/2-cup moulds and line the bases with circles of baking paper.
Melt the butter and chocolate in a pan over low heat and leave to cool.
Transfer to a bowl and stir in the sugar, eggs and vanilla. Fold in the combined flour and almonds.
Pour into the moulds and bake on a heated baking tray for 20 minutes, or until set around the edges (the centres will still be soft and fudgy).
Remove from the oven and leave for 5 minutes before turning out.
Serve with thick cream or ice cream.

Serves 4

50 g (1 3/4 oz) butter
350 g (11 oz) dark chocolate
1 cup caster sugar
4 eggs, lightly beaten
1 teaspoon vanilla essence
1/2 cup plain flour
100 g (3 1/2 oz) Vienna almonds, roughly chopped

You can store cut watermelon,
wrapped in plastic, in the fridge. It
should keep for up to a week.

watermelon, vodka and cranberry jellies

1½ leaves gelatine or 4 teaspoons
powdered gelatine
200 ml (6½ fl oz) vodka
500 ml (16 fl oz) apple and
cranberry juice
1 small watermelon

Put the gelatine in a small bowl with
3 tablespoons water and leave until
soft. Drain, if using leaf gelatine.
Put the gelatine, vodka and fruit juice in
a saucepan and stir over low heat until
the gelatine dissolves, then simmer for
2 minutes. Set aside to cool slightly.
Remove the seeds from the
watermelon and cut into small heart
shapes with a biscuit cutter.
Place some watermelon hearts in six
½-cup glasses. Pour in enough jelly to
just cover the shapes and leave in the
fridge to set.
Put more hearts into the glasses and fill
with the remaining jelly.
Chill the jellies until ready to serve.
Thread any extra hearts onto skewers,
freeze until firm and serve on the side.

Serves 6

Sencha tea is made from young green leaves and is served as a drink to welcome guests in Japan.

green tea panna cotta

Put the green tea, milk, cream and sugar in a pan and heat slowly until the sugar dissolves and the mixture is just about to boil. Remove from the heat and leave to infuse for 10 minutes. Strain the infusion back into a clean pan.
Soak the gelatine in 3 tablespoons warm water until spongy. Whisk into the cream mixture and heat gently until the gelatine has dissolved.
Pour into four lightly greased 150 ml (5 fl oz) moulds or Japanese teacups and refrigerate until set. Serve in the cups or turn out onto plates.

Serves 4

1/3 cup Japanese green tea (sencha) leaves
1 cup milk
2 cups cream
1/2 cup caster sugar
11/2 leaves gelatine or 4 teaspoons powdered gelatine

Buy young pink rhubarb stalks—
they start to become bitter and
stringy once the stems thicken.

rhubarb with vanilla and cardamom rice

1 litre milk
1 cup sugar
1 vanilla bean, split in half and seeds
scraped out
4 cardamom pods, bruised
1 cup arborio rice
200 g (6¹/2 oz) mascarpone (optional)
500 g (1 lb) rhubarb, cut into
short lengths
¹/2 cup brown sugar
1 cinnamon stick

Put the milk, sugar, vanilla bean and cardamom in a pan and heat until just about to boil.
Add the rice and cook, stirring, for 20–30 minutes, or until tender.
Add the mascarpone and beat until thick and creamy. Remove the vanilla bean and cardamom.
Put the rhubarb, brown sugar, cinnamon and 3 tablespoons water in a pan, cover with a tight-fitting lid and cook over medium heat for 5 minutes. Stir and check to see how soft the rhubarb is: it should break into strands. If it doesn't, cook for a few more minutes, taking care not to overcook or it will become mushy.
Serve with the creamed rice.

Serves 4

To harvest sunflower seeds, muslin bags are placed over the flowers to catch the seeds as they fall.

banana, sunflower and pistachio bread

Preheat the oven to 180°C (350°F/ Gas 4). Grease and line the base of a 23 cm (9 inch) loaf tin.

Beat the butter and sugar until light and creamy. Add the eggs gradually, beating well after each addition. Stir in the bananas, nuts and seeds.

Sift together the flour, bicarbonate of soda and mixed spice, then fold into the banana mixture.

Spoon into the tin and bake for 1 hour, or until a skewer comes out clean when inserted into the centre.

Leave to cool in the tin for 15 minutes before turning out onto a wire rack to cool completely.

Serve buttered and preferably drizzled with runny honey.

Serves 6–8

100 g (3 1/2 oz) butter
3/4 cup muscovado sugar
2 eggs, lightly beaten
500 g (1 lb) ripe bananas, mashed
100 g (3 1/2 oz) shelled pistachio nuts, roughly chopped
1/2 cup sunflower seeds
2 cups self-raising flour
1 teaspoon bicarbonate of soda
1/2 teaspoon mixed spice

Rose-water was widely used in the dishes of medieval England and is now prized in Middle Eastern food.

rose-water coeur à la crème with pomegranate

250 g (8 oz) ricotta cheese
1/2 cup icing sugar
1/3 cup rose-water
1 cup cream, whipped
2 oranges, peeled and cut into thick slices
1 pomegranate

Drain the ricotta cheese in muslin overnight to remove any moisture.
Put the ricotta, icing sugar and half the rose-water in a bowl and beat until smooth. Fold through the cream.
Line six coeur à la crème moulds with muslin and fill with the mixture.
Leave, covered, on a baking tray in the fridge overnight.
Turn out onto plates and serve with the orange slices, pomegranate seeds and the rest of the rose-water drizzled over the top.

Serves 6

To release the flavour, ice cream should be softened in the fridge for 30 minutes before serving.

chocky block ice cream

Place 300 g (10 oz) of the chocolate in a heatproof bowl over a pan of barely simmering water, making sure the base of the bowl is not sitting in the water. Leave until the chocolate has melted then set aside to cool.

Stir the custard and cream into the melted chocolate. Stir in the remaining chopped chocolate. Pour into an ice-cream machine and churn until frozen. (Alternatively, pour the mixture into a large metal container, cover and freeze for 2 hours, until setting around the edge. Scrape into a bowl and beat with electric beaters until smooth. Pour back into the clean metal container, cover and freeze until firm.)

Serves 6

400 g (13 oz) Belgian chocolate, roughly chopped
400 ml (13 fl oz) carton custard
300 ml (10 fl oz) cream

Buttermilk is often used in baking to incorporate air and give rise to cakes, scones and muffins.

passionfruit sugar muffins

2 1/2 cups self-raising flour
1 1/2 cups caster sugar
1 1/2 cups buttermilk
2 eggs
1 teaspoon vanilla essence
250 g (8 oz) butter, melted and cooled
1/4 cup passionfruit curd
1–2 tablespoons lemon juice

Preheat the oven to 190°C (375°F/Gas 5). Lightly grease a 12-hole 1/2-cup muffin tray. Sift the flour into a bowl and stir in 1/2 cup of the sugar. Make a well in the centre.
Whisk together the buttermilk, eggs, vanilla and 150 g (5 oz) of the melted butter and pour into the well. Stir until only just combined (the mixture should still be lumpy).
Half-fill each muffin tin with mixture, then add a teaspoon of passionfruit curd to each muffin and top up with the remaining mixture. Bake for 30 minutes, or until risen and springy to touch.
Mix the lemon juice and remaining butter in a bowl and spread the remaining sugar on a plate. Brush the warm muffins with lemon butter roll in the sugar. Repeat and serve warm.

Makes 12 muffins

Will-power will determine whether you choose the healthy or more indulgent version of these lollies.

frozen banana lollies

Roughly chop the bananas. Put the bananas, honey, yoghurt and soy milk in a blender and whizz until smooth and very thick.

Pour into ice-block trays and stand sticks upright in the centres. Freeze until solid, then rub the base of the tray with a warm damp cloth to release the lollies.

For something not quite so healthy, dip the frozen lollies in melted white chocolate, then roll in chopped pistachio nuts.

Makes about 12 lollies

4 ripe bananas
1–2 tablespoons honey
200 g (6 1/2 oz) low-fat Greek-style
    yoghurt
1 cup vanilla soy milk
500 g (1 lb) white chocoate, melted
pistachio nuts, roughly chopped

Crumble, also known as 'crisp', is
one of those delicious puddings
best served hot from the oven.

peach and plum crumbles

500 g (1 lb) ripe blood plums, halved
500 g (1 lb) ripe slipstone peaches,
halved
1/2 cup light brown sugar
100 g (3 1/2 oz) plain flour
8 amaretti biscuits, crushed
75 g (2 1/2 oz) butter, chilled and
chopped
1/4 cup sugar

Preheat the oven to 200°C (400°F/
Gas 6). Put the plum and peach halves
on a grill tray and grill until soft.
Cut the fruit into wedges and arrange in
ramekins or a large ovenproof dish.
Sprinkle lightly with the brown sugar and
toss to coat the fruit.
Mix together the flour and amaretti
biscuits in a bowl. Add the butter and
rub in with your fingertips until the
mixture resembles fine breadcrumbs.
Stir in the sugar and add 2 tablespoons
chilled water. Mix with a flat-bladed knife
until the mixture clumps in beads.
Top the fruit with the crumble and bake
for 30 minutes or until the juices from
the fruit are oozing through the crumble.

Serves 4

Native to India and Burma, the juicy aromatic mango has been termed 'fruit of the gods'.

mango lime sago

Soak the sago in cold water overnight, then drain well.

Put the sago, puréed mango, lime rind, sugar, vanilla bean and 1 cup water in a pan and stir over low heat until the sugar dissolves.

Increase the heat to medium and cook, stirring, for 10 minutes or until the sago is clear and soft. Transfer to an airtight container and refrigerate until cool. Serve in tall glasses with slices of fresh mango and lime wedges.

Serves 4

1/2 cup sago
2 cups puréed mango flesh
1 teaspoon finely grated lime rind
2 tablespoons sugar
1 vanilla bean, split in half
mango and lime wedges, to serve

Choose large heavy passionfruit
with slightly wrinkled skin—this is
a sign that the fruit is ready to eat.

passionfruit custard pots

1 cup caster sugar
4 eggs
1 cup cream
200 ml (7 fl oz) passionfruit pulp
2 tablespoons lime juice
1/2 cup sugar

Preheat the oven to 160°C (315°F/
Gas 2–3). Put the caster sugar, eggs,
cream, passionfruit pulp and lime juice
in a bowl and whisk together.
Pour the mixture into four 1-cup
ramekins and place the ramekins in a
baking dish. Pour boiling water into the
dish to come halfway up the sides of
the ramekins.
Cook for 25 minutes or until the
custards are set. Remove from the
dish and allow to cool. Refrigerate for
4 hours before serving.
Put the sugar in a pan over low heat
until melted and starting to turn liquid.
Bring slowly to the boil, then boil until
deep caramel colour. Pour over the
custard pots to cover the surface.
Leave to cool and set (don't refrigerate).

Serves 4

irish coffee semifreddo with praline shards

Put the egg yolks, whisky, coffee and half the sugar in a heatproof bowl and beat over a pan of simmering water until the mixture is thick and pale. Remove from the heat to cool. Whisk the egg whites in a clean dry bowl until soft peaks form. Gradually beat in the remaining sugar until the mixture is thick and glossy. Fold the egg whites and cream into the cooled mixture and pour into a 23 cm (9 inch) loaf tin. Cover with plastic wrap and freeze until firm. To make the praline, put the nuts and mint leaves on a large tray lined with baking paper. Put the sugar and 3 tablespoons water in a pan and stir over low heat until the sugar dissolves. Bring to the boil and boil until deep golden brown. Pour over the nuts and mint, then press on some lavender flowers. Leave to cool, then break into large shards. Serve slices of the semifreddo with shards of praline.

Serves 4–6

4 egg yolks
1/4 cup whisky
1 tablespoon finely ground coffee
1 cup caster sugar
2 egg whites
300 ml (10 fl oz) cream, whipped

Praline
125 g (4 oz) shelled pistachio nuts
1 tablespoon fresh mint leaves
1 cup sugar
1 tablespoon fresh lavender flowers

Date palms can live for a century and yield up to 45 kg of fruit per year. That's a lot of puddings.

gooey date pudding

2 1/2 cups chopped pitted dates
1 teaspoon ground ginger
1 1/2 teaspoons bicarbonate of soda
1 teaspoon vanilla essence
150 g (5 oz) butter
3/4 cup caster sugar
3 eggs, lightly beaten
1 3/4 cups self-raising flour

Sauce
2 cups cream
2 cups brown sugar
2 tablespoons brandy (optional)

Preheat the oven to 180°C (350°F/ Gas 4). Grease and line the base of a 20 cm (8 inch) square cake tin.
Put the dates, ginger and 2 cups water in a pan and bring to the boil. Reduce the heat and simmer for 5 minutes. Remove from the heat and stir in the bicarbonate of soda and vanilla. Cool. Beat the butter and sugar until light and creamy. Add the eggs gradually, beating well after each addition.
Fold in the flour and the date mixture, then pour into the tin. Bake for 1 hour, or until a skewer comes out clean when inserted into the centre of the pudding.
To make the sauce, put the cream, sugar and brandy in a pan. Bring to the boil, stirring, then simmer for 5 minutes or until thick enough to coat a spoon. Serve with the pudding and cream.

Serves 8

pavlovas with lemon curd and tropical fruit

Preheat the oven to 150°C (300°F/ Gas 2). Beat the egg whites in a clean dry bowl until soft peaks form. Add the sugar gradually, beating well after each addition, until thick and glossy with stiff peaks. Stir in the vanilla.

Line a tray with baking paper and spoon the mixture into six small nests on the tray. Bake for 20 minutes, then reduce the oven to 120°C (250°F/Gas 1/2) and bake for 10 minutes. Turn off the oven and leave the pavlovas to cool in the oven with the door ajar.

To make the lemon curd, put the rind, juice, sugar, eggs and butter in a heatproof bowl and whisk together. Place the bowl over a pan of barely simmering water, making sure the base of the bowl is not sitting in the water. Stir for about 15 minutes, or until the curd is thick—do not allow it to boil. Lay plastic wrap on the surface and leave to cool.

Fold the whipped cream through the curd. Spoon into the pavlovas and top with banana, mango and passionfruit.

Serves 6

4 egg whites
1 cup caster sugar
1 teaspoon vanilla essence

Lemon curd
1 tablespoon grated lemon rind
2 tablespoons lemon juice
1/4 cup caster sugar
2 eggs
50 g (1 3/4 oz) butter
1 cup cream, whipped
2 bananas, sliced
1 mango, sliced
8 passionfruit

Macadamias are sweet buttery nuts native to Australia. Store in an airtight container in the fridge.

macadamia golden syrup dumplings

1 cup self-raising flour
1/2 teaspoon ground cinnamon
40 g (11/4 oz) butter, chilled and chopped
100 g (31/2 oz) macadamia nuts, roasted and roughly chopped
1 egg, lightly beaten
1 tablespoon milk

Syrup
1 cup demerara sugar
40 g (11/4 oz) butter
3 tablespoons golden syrup
2 tablespoons dark rum
2 tablespoons lemon juice

Sift the flour and cinnamon into a bowl. Add the butter and rub in with your fingertips until the mixture resembles fine breadcrumbs. Stir in the nuts. Add the combined egg and milk and mix to form a soft dough.
To make the syrup, put the sugar, butter, syrup, rum, lemon juice and 2 cups water in a saucepan and stir over low heat until the sugar dissolves. Drop large spoonfuls of the dough into the simmering liquid and cook, covered, for 10 minutes, or until a skewer comes out clean when inserted into the centre of a dumpling. Serve with thick cream.

Serves 4

This is one of those foolproof
throw-it-all-in kind of cakes,
delicious either warm or cold.

chocolate cake with drunken muscatels

Preheat the oven to 180°C (350°F
Gas 4). Grease and line a deep 20 cm
(8 inch) round cake tin.
Put the muscatels and muscat in a pan
and bring to the boil. Remove from the
heat and leave for 4 hours.
Put the sugar, flour, cocoa, bicarbonate
of soda, oil, eggs and buttermilk in a
bowl and beat until smooth.
Spoon into the tin and bake for
40 minutes, or until a skewer comes
out clean when inserted into the centre.
Cool in the tin for 10 minutes before
turning out onto a wire rack.
To make the sauce, put the chocolate
and cream in a pan and heat gently,
stirring, until melted and combined.
Drizzle over the cake and serve with the
drunken muscatels and thick cream.

Serves 6–8

200 g (6 1/2 oz) muscatel grapes
375 ml (12 fl oz) muscat
1 cup caster sugar
1 3/4 cups self-raising flour
1 cup cocoa powder
1 teaspoon bicarbonate of soda
1/4 cup vegetable oil
2 eggs, lightly beaten
3/4 cup buttermilk

Chocolate sauce
250 g (8 oz) dark chocolate, chopped
1 cup cream

It is the little pieces of broken
meringue that give this easy
custard ice cream its chewiness.

chewy coconut and star anise ice cream

500 ml (16 fl oz) coconut cream
6 star anise
2 stalks lemongrass, halved
600 ml (20 fl oz) carton custard
10 small meringues, roughly chopped

Put the coconut cream, star anise and
lemongrass in a pan and bring just to
the boil. Remove from the heat and
leave to cool. Remove the lemongrass.
Combine with the custard, then transfer
to an ice-cream machine and churn
until almost firm.
(Alternatively, pour the mixture into a
large metal container, cover and freeze
for 2 hours, until setting around the
edge. Scrape into a bowl and beat
until smooth. Pour back into the clean
metal container, cover and freeze until
almost firm.)
Stir the meringues through the ice
cream and return to the freezer. Keep
frozen but soften in the fridge for
30 minutes before serving.
Serve in cones or tall glasses, layered
with tropical fruit.

Serves 4–6

For the best chocolate-chip cookies, use the best chocolate: Belgian couverture.

the ultimate chocolate-chip cookie

Preheat the oven to 180°C (350°F Gas 4). Beat the butter, sugar and vanilla until light and creamy. Beat in the egg.
Stir in the sifted flour and baking powder and fold through the white and dark chocolate chunks.
Spoon heaped tablespoons of the mixture onto a non-stick baking tray, leaving room for spreading. Flatten slightly and bake for 10–15 minutes or until browning around the edges. Cool for 2 minutes on the tray before transferring to a wire rack.

Makes 12 large cookies

150 g (5 oz) butter, softened
1 cup brown sugar
1 teaspoon vanilla essence
1 egg, lightly beaten
1 1/2 cups plain flour
1/2 teaspoon baking powder
50 g (1 3/4 oz) white chocolate, cut into chunks
200 g (6 1/2 oz) dark chocolate, cut into chunks

As a variation, try ricotta in place
of ice cream. And mango or
banana instead of the berries.

fried ice cream and berry sandwiches

4 vanilla ice cream bars
300 g (10 oz) mixed berries
8 thick slices white bread
50 g (1³/4 oz) butter, softened

Cut the ice cream into 1 cm (¹/2 inch)
thick slices and place on a paper-lined
tray in the freezer until very firm.
If you are using large berries, such as
strawberries, cut them into thick slices.
Place a slice or two of ice cream onto a
piece of bread, top with some berries
and sandwich with another slice of
bread. Put back in the freezer until the
ice cream is very firm again.
Heat the butter in a non-stick frying pan
and cook the sandwiches, in batches if
your pan isn't big enough, until crisp
and golden on both sides.

Serves 4

Make sure you use the soft silken tofu for this recipe—the firmer types have much too strong a flavour.

tofu with lemongrass and lime syrup

Put the sugar and 1 cup water in a pan and stir over low heat until dissolved. Add the lemongrass and lime leaves and bring to the boil. Boil for 5 minutes, or until slightly thickened. Leave to cool. Cut the tofu into four blocks and carefully place in serving bowls. Arrange the fruit beside the tofu and drizzle the syrup over the top. Great with coconut ice cream.

Serves 4

1 cup grated light palm sugar
1–2 stalks lemongrass, split in half lengthways
2 kaffir lime leaves, finely shredded
500 g (1 lb) silken tofu
1/2 red papaya, cut into wedges
2 kiwifruit, peeled and sliced
12 fresh lychees or rambutans

Using brioche for your eggy bread puts a new adult spin on the traditional nursery favourite.

brioche eggy bread with figs and raspberry cream

4 small brioche
3 eggs, lightly beaten
1 cup milk
1 teaspoon almond essence
50 g (1³/4 oz) butter
6 ripe figs, halved
2 tablespoons brown sugar

Raspberry cream
200 g (6¹/2 oz) raspberries
200 g (6¹/2 oz) sour cream
3 tablespoons brown sugar

Cut the brioche lengthways into thick slices. Whisk together the eggs, milk and almond essence.

Heat half the butter in a large frying pan, dip a slice of brioche in the egg mixture, letting any extra drain off, then lay in the pan. Fry over medium heat until golden brown on both sides. Keep warm while you cook the rest, adding more butter to the pan as you need it. Arrange the figs, cut side up, on a baking tray, sprinkle lightly with the sugar and grill until the sugar has caramelized and the figs have softened. To make the raspberry cream, lightly crush the raspberries with a fork. Stir through the sour cream with the brown sugar. Serve with the brioche and figs.

Serves 4

Test star anise for freshness by
squeezing a segment until the
seeds pop. The aroma is instant.

poached stone fruits

1 cup caster sugar
1 cinnamon stick
3 star anise
6 cloves
500 g (1 lb) apricots
1 kg (2 lb) slipstone peaches
500 g (1 lb) nectarines

Put the sugar, cinnamon, star anise and
cloves in a large pan with 1 litre water
and stir over low heat until the sugar
has dissolved.
Bring to the boil, add the fruit and
simmer for 10 minutes or until soft.
Remove the fruit, peel and halve.
Simmer the liquid for 10 minutes, or
until thickened slightly.
Place the fruit in a bowl, pour the syrup
over the top and leave to cool. Store in
a vacuum-sealed glass jar in the fridge
for up to 3 weeks.
Delicious with thick yoghurt or on top of
breakfast cereals.

Serves 6–8

Pandoro is a rich Italian bread
served during the festive season.
If you can't find it, use panettone.

chocolate cherry italian pudding

1 large pandoro, thickly sliced
125 g (4 oz) dark chocolate, chopped
400 g (13 oz) morello cherries,
drained, syrup reserved
4 eggs
1/3 cup caster sugar
1 cup milk
1 cup cream
1/2 cup caster sugar, extra
1/4 cup kirsch
150 g (5 oz) fresh cherries

Preheat the oven to 180°C (350°F/
Gas 4). Grease and line a 20 cm
(8 inch) round springform tin and wrap
foil around the base to prevent leaks.
Layer the pandoro slices in the tin with
the chocolate and morello cherries.
Whisk together the eggs, sugar, milk
and cream and pour over the pandoro.
Leave to stand for 10 minutes.
Bake for 45 minutes, or until a skewer
comes out clean when inserted into
the centre. Leave for 10 minutes.
Put the syrup reserved from the
cherries in a pan with the extra sugar,
kirsch and 1 cup water and stir over
low heat until the sugar dissolves. Bring
to the boil and cook without stirring until
the sauce reduces and thickens.
Serve the pudding in wedges with the
cherry syrup and fresh cherries.

Serves 6–8

These melt-in-your-mouth biscuits will keep for a couple of weeks in an airtight container.

powdered greek shortbreads

Preheat the oven to 180°C (350°F/ Gas 4). Scatter the almonds over a non-stick baking tray and bake for 5 minutes or until lightly golden. Leave to cool and then chop finely.

Beat the butter and 3 tablespoons icing sugar until light and creamy. Beat in the rose-water and lime rind.

Sift together the flour and allspice, add the almonds, then lightly fold into the mixture until a smooth dough forms. Shape tablespoons of the mixture into moon shapes on two non-stick baking trays. Bake for 15–20 minutes, or until lightly golden, then transfer to a wire rack and leave to cool completely. Transfer to a flat container and dredge with the remaining sifted icing sugar.

Makes about 28 biscuits

125 g (4 oz) blanched almonds
250 g (8 oz) butter, cubed and softened
41/4 cups icing sugar
1 tablespoon rose-water
1 teaspoon finely grated lime rind
21/2 cups plain flour
1 teaspoon ground allspice

christmas pudding with aniseed custard

1 cup self-raising flour
1 teaspoon grated nutmeg
1 teaspoon mixed spice
2 cups fresh breadcrumbs
200 g (6¹/2 oz) macadamia nuts,
toasted and roughly chopped
250 g (8 oz) dried apricots
500 g (1 lb) dried mixed fruit
200 g (6¹/2 oz) chopped dried figs
100 g (3¹/2 oz) raisins
100 g (3¹/2 oz) sultanas
3 eggs, lightly beaten
375 ml (12 fl oz) Guinness
1/3 cup brandy

Aniseed custard
5 egg yolks
1/3 cup caster sugar
2 teaspoons cornflour
300 ml (10 fl oz) cream
300 ml (10 fl oz) milk
1 vanilla bean, halved
30 g (1 oz) aniseed, lightly crushed or
2 teaspoons liquid aniseed

Sift the flour and spices into a bowl, add the breadcrumbs, nuts and all the dried fruit and mix together. Whisk the eggs, Guinness and brandy. Add to the bowl. Beat thoroughly for 5 minutes, or until the mixture is quite thick but drops off a spoon. Cover and leave overnight.
Lightly grease two 1-litre or four 500-ml (16 fl oz) pudding basins. Spoon the mixture into the basins. Cover the surface with lightly greased baking paper and a large piece of calico. Secure the cloth around the rim with string, then fold over the top and tie the opposite corners together on top of the pudding.
Put the puddings in a large pan with water to reach halfway up the side of the basins, cover and steam for 5 hours, checking the water every half hour.
For the custard, whisk the yolks, sugar and cornflour. Put the cream, milk, vanilla bean and aniseed in a pan and heat just to boiling point. Cool for 5 minutes, then whisk into the egg mixture. Cook in a clean pan, stirring, until thickened. Strain and serve with the pudding.

Serves about 20

Published by Murdoch Books®,
a division of Murdoch Magazines Pty Ltd,
GPO Box 1203, Sydney, NSW Australia 2001.

Recipes: Jody Vassallo
Photographer: Chris Chen
Stylist: Michelle Noerianto
Home Economist: Valli Little
Concept & Design: Marylouise Brammer
Project Manager: Anna Waddington
Editor: Jane Price
Recipe Testing: Valli Little, Jody Vassallo

Chief Executive: Mark Smith
Publisher: Kay Scarlett
Production Manager: Liz Fitzgerald

National Library of Australia Cataloguing-in-Publication Data
Vassallo, Jody. marie claire Sweet.
ISBN 1 74045 089 2
1. Desserts. 2. Confectionery. I. Chen, Chris. II. Title.
(Series: marie claire style).
641.86

Published by:
AUSTRALIA
Murdoch Books® Australia
GPO Box 1203
Sydney NSW 2001
Phone: (612) 8220 2000
Fax: (612) 8220 2558

UK
Murdoch Books® UK
Ferry House,
51–57 Lacy Road
London SW15 1PR
Phone: (020) 8355 1480
Fax: (020) 8355 1499

Printed by Toppan Printing Hong Kong Co. Ltd. PRINTED IN CHINA. First printed 2001.
© Design Murdoch Books® 2001. © Text Jody Vassallo.© Photography Chris Chen.